Jane Eyre

Adapted by Mary Sebag-Montefiore
Illustrated by Alan Marks

Reading consultant: Alison Kelly
University of Roehampton

Designed by Caroline Spatz
Series editor: Lesley Sims
Series designer: Russell Punter

First published in 2012 by Usborne Publishing Ltd.,
Usborne House, 83-85 Saffron Hill, London
EC1N 8RT, England. www.usborne.com

Copyright © 2012 Usborne Publishing Ltd.
The name Usborne and the devices 🐝 ♀ are
Trade Marks of Usborne Publishing Ltd.
All rights reserved. No part of this publication may be
reproduced, stored in a retrieval system or transmitted
in any form or by any means, electronic, mechanical,
photocopying, recording or otherwise, without
the prior permission of the publisher.
UE First published in America in 2012

Contents

Chapter 1	The red room	4
Chapter 2	School	8
Chapter 3	The rider in the moonlight	18
Chapter 4	A fire is lit	26
Chapter 5	Lose the world for love	38
Chapter 6	The voice from nowhere	55

Chapter 1
The red room

"Where's Jane? I know... hidden behind the curtain, like a little rat!" Flinging back the curtain, my cousin John revealed me, clinging to the window seat.

"There she is," he crowed to his sisters, Eliza and Georgiana. "Come out... NOW!" And he grabbed my book, my beloved *History of Birds*. I loved imagining myself into its tales of faraway lands, they seemed so lonely, yet mysterious...

I quickly obeyed John, dreading his violent temper.

"This is MY book, not yours," sneered John, as I stood in front of him, trembling. "You have NOTHING, orphan!"

He hurled the book at my head.

I ducked – but not quickly enough. Blood trickled down my neck, and a sharp pain turned my terror to anger. I flew at him, crying, "You're like the cruel Roman emperors!"

I don't know what my hands did; I was ten and he a heavy, flabby fourteen-year-old, but he bellowed like a baby.

My Aunt Reed, hearing the commotion, ordered her servants to come. "Take her to the red room and lock her in there."

I fought like a wildcat all the way, until they threw me inside and shut the door.

The red room was never slept in. It was here that my uncle had died and lain in state until he was borne away in his coffin. Here was a vast bed with massive pillars; on the floor, a red carpet; the windows dark with blinds drawn down. This chilly chamber never even saw a fire.

Despairingly, I tried the door... Locked. With nothing else to do, I sat on a stool and thought about my life. Why did they hate me so?

My cousins were spoiled, selfish bullies, yet they were adored. I could never please them or Aunt Reed. 'Naughty, sullen, ugly,' they called me, and I...? I could not love them. In that house, I was an outsider.

"Not fair! Not fair!" raged my heart.

Hours passed. I tried to face the darkness boldly – until I saw a moving light. I think now it was the gleam from some distant lantern, but in my gloomy prison, I thought it a vision from another world, my Uncle Reed's ghost. A rushing noise filled my ears. I screamed.

Aunt Reed opened the door, her gown rustling stormily.

"Oh Aunt, please..." I clung to her hands, "punish me another way. I can't bear this."

"Silence, Jane!" Thrusting me back, she locked the door once more. As the key turned, I sank into unconsciousness. The memory – the agony – of that night has never left me.

Chapter 2
School

A week later, Aunt Reed summoned me to her room, where a strange man glared at me. "This, Mr. Brocklehurst, is Jane Eyre. Her mother was my dead husband's sister. She has no claim on me."

What enormous teeth he had! And a huge nose and mouth.

"You are bad, I hear," he trumpeted. "Deceitful. How can you avoid hell, where naughty children burn forever?"

"I must keep well and not die."

"Bad indeed! A good child would say, 'I will behave well.' Yes, Mrs. Reed, she may go to my school. She will learn humility."

He departed, leaving me with Aunt Reed. "Go upstairs," she said, not even looking at me.

But I had to speak out. "I am not deceitful," I began. "You think I have no feelings, that I can do without one bit of love or kindness, but I can't live like that. You have no pity in your heart. People think you are a good, kind woman, but I'll tell everyone at this school that it is you who is bad and deceitful…"

It was my first victory. Aunt Reed left the room without a word.

I journeyed to school alone, the horse and cart whirling me fifty miles away. On arrival, I was taken to a dark, icy room lit by two candles. Seated on benches were rows of girls wearing thin brown cotton frocks, light pinafores, their hair pulled back tightly. Supper was served: nasty-tasting water and broken, thin oatcakes.

Too tired to eat, I was sent to a cold dormitory with long lines of beds. Too weary to fear the strangeness, I slept.

A clanging bell woke us. Shivering, we rose to wash, but the basin in the middle of the room was filled with ice.

An hour and a half of prayers followed, then... how welcome: breakfast. Ravenous, I gulped my first mouthful – and put down my spoon, revolted. Burned porridge! I saw each girl try and fail to swallow her food. Breakfast was over, and none had eaten.

After my first three lessons of History, Arithmetic and Geography, I was shivering with cold and hunger, like everyone else.

One girl was picked on constantly by Miss Scatcherd, the teacher. "Helen Burns, hold up your head. Helen Burns, your nails are dirty. Have you not washed?"

"Why doesn't Helen explain?" I thought. "She couldn't because there was no water."

"Fetch the rod, you filthy child."

Miss Scatcherd beat her neck with quick, hard strokes. Not a tear rose in Helen's eyes.

"How could you bear to be beaten?" I asked her at playtime. "I couldn't."

"Yes, you could. It's weak to say you can't bear what you have to."

"But it was unfair."

"N-no," said Helen. "I have faults. I'm untidy. I read when I should learn my lessons. I know I annoy Miss Scatcherd."

"Don't you hate her?" I said. "I hate anyone who dislikes me."

"That's just wrong. Read the Bible."

"Why? What does it say?"

Helen smiled. "Love your enemies."

"Huh," I snorted. "That means I should love Aunt Reed and John," and I told Helen about them. "Don't you think they're cruel?" I asked impatiently.

"You'd be happier if you tried to forget them," said Helen. "Life's too short to hold a grudge about past wrongs."

Never had I met anyone so gentle, so good. And her smile! I remember it still, how it lit up her thin face, like the reflection of an angel. She coughed, put her arm around me, and we went inside.

Three weeks later, Mr. Brocklehurst visited the school.

"Where is the new pupil, Jane Eyre?" he asked. "Place her upon this chair."

In view of the entire school, I stood.

"This child," Mr. Brocklehurst announced, "is a LIAR! Her aunt, an excellent lady, was forced to remove her from her own children lest she infect them with her badness. Avoid Jane Eyre! Let her stand here in disgrace all afternoon."

Helen was with me when I got off that chair, wretched with embarrassment.

"Everyone will hate me," I sobbed.

"No, Jane," she insisted. "No one here likes Mr. Brocklehurst. He's the one who provides the poor food, our thin clothes and this icy building. Just do your best and people will believe in you, not Mr. Brocklehurst's words."

She calmed me, but her cough, I noticed, was worse. Many of the girls had bad coughs now.

As the freezing months drew to spring, half the school became ill. Some lay in bed; those who were not orphans went home.

Typhus fever raged through the school.

It was inflamed by our half-starvation, the unclean water we drank, the cold, and the fetid air of our institution. I had not seen Helen for weeks. I was told she was desperately ill.

"May I visit her?" I asked Miss Scatcherd.

"Oh no. You'll catch the fever."

But I had to see her. So, one night, I crept into every bedroom until I found her.

"Jane," she whispered, smiling.

She'll get better, I thought. She couldn't sound so calm, so happy... if...

"You've come to say goodbye..."

A terrible fit of coughing silenced her, making me cry, "Don't die, Helen, don't go... Where will you go?"

"Don't be unhappy, Jane," she murmured. "I believe I am going to God."

"But where is God?" I demanded. "What is God?"

"I believe we find out, that we go to a place of happiness."

I felt as if I couldn't let her go. Presently, she said in her sweet voice, "Stay with me. I like you here."

"Dear Helen." I hugged her.

"I'm sleepy now... it's comfortable with you here. Goodnight, Jane."

"Goodnight, Helen."

We slept. When I awoke, we were lying with our arms clasped around each other, but Helen was perfectly still.

Chapter 3
The rider in the moonlight

So many children died, it caused a great scandal, and Mr. Brocklehurst was held responsible. Soon after, everything changed. The school moved to a better building; the food improved, our clothes were warmer, and we had new teachers, who were kind and inspiring. I stayed there for six years as a pupil, and two as a teacher myself. I was happy enough, until restlessness overcame me.

I wanted change – new faces, new circumstances. I decided to advertise for a position as a governess. My advertisement was answered. A Mrs. Fairfax of Thornfield Hall, seventy miles away, wanted my services for a little girl named Adèle.

There I went, half thrilled by my adventure, half anxious at what lay ahead.

Thornfield Hall rose three floors high, topped with battlements where rooks flew in and out. In the distance, a ring of hills gave it a quiet, lonely air. Inside, the hall and gallery were more like a church than a house – vast, dark and eerie.

"Hello, my dear," Mrs. Fairfax greeted me when I arrived. "Let me show you your room."

She treats me as a visitor, not a servant, I thought, gratefully. My room, down a long corridor, breathed luxury to me. After unpacking, I asked to meet my pupil, Adèle Fairfax.

"Oh, she's not my daughter," said Mrs. Fairfax, with a smile. "She's French. She's Mr. Rochester's ward."

"Who is Mr. Rochester?"

"Why, he owns Thornfield."

"I thought it belonged to you."

"Oh no!" She laughed. "I'm the housekeeper. We live quietly here," she added. "Just Adèle, Grace Poole – the upstairs servant – and other servants, of course. Mr. Rochester travels abroad. He seldom comes home."

A little girl entered the room, about seven years old, with curls to her waist.

"Bonjour Adèle," I said.

She replied in a gabble of French, which I, well-taught at school, understood easily. She offered to sing and dance for me and our bond grew from there. I quickly became fond of her and enjoyed my work but I was puzzled by Mr. Rochester's absence.

I asked Mrs. Fairfax about him – it seemed so strange to own a home like Thornfield and not be in it.

"He's clever," she began, "but peculiar."

"In what way?" I asked.

"You can't make out if he's joking or serious, or even pleased. I don't really understand him."

We were upstairs as we spoke, walking along the corridor to my room. At the end was an attic staircase leading to the third floor. From above came a sound – the last I expected to hear – a laugh. It stopped, and began again, a low, mirthless laugh that echoed into every corner.

"What is that?" I exclaimed.

"Grace Poole," said Mrs. Fairfax quickly. "She sometimes sews in the attics. Grace!" she called.

I expected no answer. The noise was too ghostly for human lips, but a door opened and a woman came down the attic stairs, a squat figure, utterly unlike the phantom of my imagination.

"Too much noise, Grace," Mrs. Fairfax said.

Grace, nodding silently, plodded back upstairs.

October, November, December passed. In January, Adèle had a cold, and I gave her a break from lessons, wishing I'd had such treats in my childhood. It was a fine, cold day, and I went on an afternoon walk.

I meandered in the lanes, watching the early moon rise pale above the branches, listening to rippling streams flowing through the dales. As the sky darkened, I saw a dog gliding ghost-like past the hazel trees, then a horse, and on its back, a rider.

He passed; I went on, telling myself this eerie vision was merely someone out for a ride. I heard then a sliding sound, a tumble, a volley of shouting. Man and horse had slipped on a sheet of ice, and the man was thrown.

I rushed over. "Can I help?" I asked.

"Who the deuce are you?"

"I am the governess at Thornfield Hall."

"Ah! The governess! I had forgotten. Take my horse's bridle and lead him to me, if you are not afraid."

The horse bucked and reared. I was terrified.

"You'll never do it," the man laughed. His hair was black, his face decisive, his mouth, chin and jaw grim, despite his laughter. "Come here instead."

Leaning hard on me, he limped to the horse, sprang into his saddle, grimacing, and rode away.

When I got back to Thornfield, the servants were rushing about like crazy things. All the lights blazed in every room; all fires burned brightly.

"Mr. Rochester has arrived," gasped Mrs. Fairfax.

Chapter 4
A fire is lit

The next day, Mrs. Fairfax told me that Mr. Rochester wished to see me in the library. The dog I'd seen earlier basked by the fire, Adèle stroking him. In the chair, firelight shining on his face, was the rider of yesterday.

"Mon cadeau," Adèle was pleading.

"Your present is upstairs. Wait," he ordered.

"Do you have a present for Miss Eyre also?"

"Do you expect one, Miss Eyre?" His eyes, I saw, were dark and piercing.

"No sir."

"I've been questioning Adèle," he said. "I find you've much improved her."

"Sir, that is my present," I replied, "your praise of her progress."

"Hmph! What are your talents?" he asked abruptly. "Do you play the piano?"

"A little."

"Play now."

I did so…

"Enough! You certainly play a little, not well, but passable. Do you draw? Paint?"

I showed him my portfolio. He examined my paintings, one of clouds over a stormy sea, another of a dark blue twilight sky in which you could just see a woman's shape, her eyes wild, and lastly, an iceberg piercing a sky lit by northern lights.

"Were you happy when you painted these?" he inquired.

"Happy enough."

"Have you seen these places in dreams? What is their meaning?"

He caught my gaze as I put the pictures away, without answering.

"You're studying me. Do you think me handsome?"

"No, sir," I replied.

"You are unusual," he declared. "You appear quiet, serious, self-effacing even, yet you're direct. You look puzzled, Miss Eyre, but puzzlement becomes you. Are you hurt? What are you thinking?"

"That few masters would care if their servants were hurt by their words."

"I like your honesty," he said.

Ringing a bell, he told a servant to fetch Adèle's present. Eagerly she unwrapped a pink silk dress, a wreath of rosebuds, a pair of satin shoes.

"Ah! I shall be très belle!" Adèle flitted away to try them on.

He told me then her history. She was the unwanted daughter of a French dancer he'd befriended. Feeling sorry for the neglected child, he offered to take her and give her an English country upbringing. Adèle's mother had given her away without a backward glance.

"Now you know her unlovely background, you'll leave us, I expect."

"No, sir. How could I prefer some pampered rich pet to this lonely waif? I care for her more than ever."

As the days slipped by, my life changed. Reader, I had never been as happy. Mr. Rochester was moody, proud, sometimes bitter, but to me, a friend always. His presence warmed me more than the brightest fire. Mrs. Fairfax said he never stayed at Thornfield more than two weeks, yet two months rushed past…

One night, I woke to hear a sound, like fingers groping at the panels outside my door. "Who's there?" I called. No answer. I was chilled with fear. Then a demonic laugh at the keyhole. Grace Poole, I remembered, laughed like that. It was impossible to remain in bed. Opening my door, I saw a candle left on the matting outside, and the air dim with smoke pouring from Mr. Rochester's bedroom.

I ran in. His bed was ablaze.

"Wake up!" I cried, but smoke had stupefied him. I seized a jug of water, hurled it in his face, and managed to quench the flames.

"You're drowning me," he spluttered, as he came to.

"Sir, there's been a fire," I gasped. "Shall I call Mrs. Fairfax?"

"Let her sleep. I must visit the third floor." Fully awake now, he sprang out of bed, pausing to take my hand in both his own. "I owe you my life, Jane. I knew you would do me good. Your eyes told me so when first we met."

"I heard a laugh, sir. Grace Poole laughs that way."

But he dismissed it. "Forget it. Say nothing about the fire, Jane."

Next day, as the servants talked of how Mr. Rochester's candle had set his bed curtains alight, I saw Grace stolidly cleaning the smoke-grimed windows.

I didn't trust her. I said, to test her, "Last night I heard a strange laugh."

"You were dreaming," she insisted. "Still, you should lock your door, miss."

I was amazed by her hypocrisy. I longed to ask Mr. Rochester why he employed her. He must realize she was dangerous; why keep it secret? I knew if my curiosity irritated him, I could soothe him. We had fallen into a way of speaking together that suited us both. I would hover on the brink of going too far, treating it like a game of skill and delighting in it.

Shortly after the fire, he left Thornfield for a while. Without him, the house seemed empty. He'd gone to a grand house-party nearby, Mrs. Fairfax told me, where a Miss Blanche Ingram was staying. I'd heard Miss Ingram was beautiful and that Mr. Rochester admired her greatly. Despair filled my heart.

"You're a fool!" I rebuked myself, when

I was alone. "Did you think he liked you? He praised your eyes, did he? Open them, see your senselessness! How could you, the governess, be preferred to a rich lady?"

Adèle and I busied ourselves in the quiet house. Then suddenly it burst into activity. The servants whipped dust covers off the furniture, polished silver and piled exotic flowers in vases.

"Mr. Rochester is bringing guests to stay, including Miss Ingram," said Mrs. Fairfax.

I took Adèle into the drawing room to greet them. Blanche Ingram was as I'd imagined her, majestic and haughty, admired by all. And Mr. Rochester? He seemed so distant from me. I stole secret glances at him, stab-wounds of painful pleasure.

"What a little darling!" Blanche Ingram exclaimed when she saw Adèle. "Why not send her to school, Mr. Rochester? I must have had a dozen governesses as a child, all detestable and ridiculous."

I read her character during this visit. She was showy, not genuine, and spiteful to Adèle. I saw Mr. Rochester did not love her, but – and this tortured me – would marry her because of her family connections and rank.

Reader, I loved him. Though he'd ceased to notice me, I could not unlove him now.

Chapter 5
Lose the world for love

The guests left and a new visitor came unexpectedly to Thornfield, a Mr. Mason from the West Indies. I saw Mr. Rochester's face grow white. I heard him mutter, "I never thought he'd come here." I heard Mr. Mason demand, "Take me to her." Her? What did he mean?

He left, and Mr. Rochester led me to the garden seat beneath the chestnut tree.

"I wish I were on a quiet island with only you, Jane. If all my friends sneered at me and dropped me, what would you do?"

"I'd stay with you."

"You'd suffer for my sake?"

"I would, sir."

"Suppose, Jane, you were not yourself, but a wild boy. Imagine yourself in a foreign land, pretend there you made a hideous mistake, the result of which must ruin your existence forever. You are bitter, unhappy, then you make a new friend. You want to start again, make a new life. Wouldn't you ignore an obstacle that stands between you and happiness?"

What could I say? The wind whispered, the birds sang their song, but answer had I none.

"It's time to move on," he said.

This was it. The blow was coming. "Are you going to be married, sir?" I asked.

"Exactly. You've hit the nail on the head."

I sobbed; I could take no more. "Here at Thornfield I've found happiness. Now I know you, Mr. Rochester, the thought of being torn from you is like facing death."

"Why should you be torn away?"

"Because of your bride..."

"No, you must stay, Jane."

"I must GO," I cried. "How can I stay and be nothing to you? Do you think I am without feelings? Do you think, because I am poor, obscure, plain and little, that I have no heart and soul? No! I have as much soul and heart as you, and if I had wealth or beauty, I should make it as hard for you to leave me as it is now for me to leave you."

"Jane," he interrupted, "it is you I want to marry."

I was silent.

"Do you doubt me?"

"Entirely."

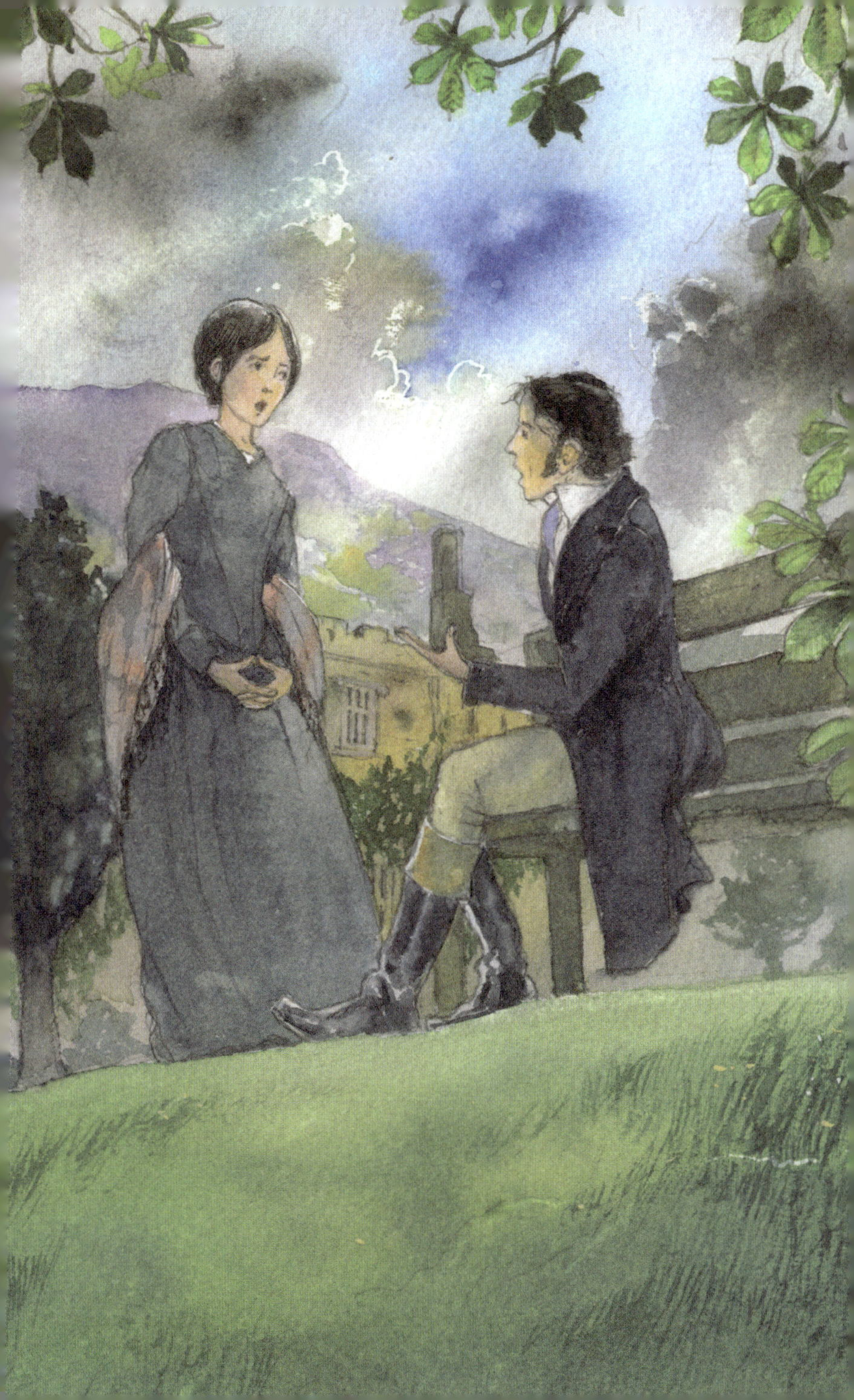

"You think I love Blanche Ingram? You're wrong! You I love as my own flesh. I entreat you, accept me." Wildly, he added, "Say my name, Edward. Say, 'Edward, I will marry you'."

"Dear Edward. I will."

He laid his cheek on mine. "God pardon me. Let no man interfere."

Night came on, quickly and violently. As we sat there, the chestnut tree writhed and groaned in the wind. A searing flash leaped from the dark clouds, a peal of thunder rattled and the rain rushed down, sending us inside.

In the morning I saw the tree had been struck by lightning and was split in two.

I wondered if Mr. Rochester's proposal had been a dream, until I saw the mirror reflect my rosy cheeks, my eyes bright with hope, and heard him renew his words of love.

"I'll shower you with jewels," he promised, "give you a priceless veil."

"I don't need jewels or fine clothes."

"Four weeks today, and you'll be mine."

Mrs. Fairfax was amazed to hear our news, and doubtful. "No equality of fortune or position," she said. "Are you sure?"

I grew irritated with her, preferring Adèle's undisguised delight.

Mr. Rochester planned to take me away the very moment the ceremony was over, and travel abroad.

"Please God this is the last meal but one you will eat at Thornfield," he said at supper, the night before our wedding. "But what's the matter, Jane? You look worried."

"I had a dream last night," I murmured. "At least, I *think* it was a dream…"

"Tell me," he demanded.

"I dreamed that Thornfield was a ruin, haunted by bats and owls and that you were far away. Then I woke, to a gleam of candlelight. Someone opened my wardrobe where I'd hung my wedding dress, not Mrs. Fairfax, nor Grace Poole, but a tall woman with wild, thick, dark hair. She ripped my wedding veil asunder, then came over and thrust her candle in my face. Oh! Her features were terrible… savage… her eyes rolling. Who or what was she?"

"It was only a dream, Jane." He flung his arms around me. "You're safe." And then he seemed to mutter, "Thank God only the veil was harmed."

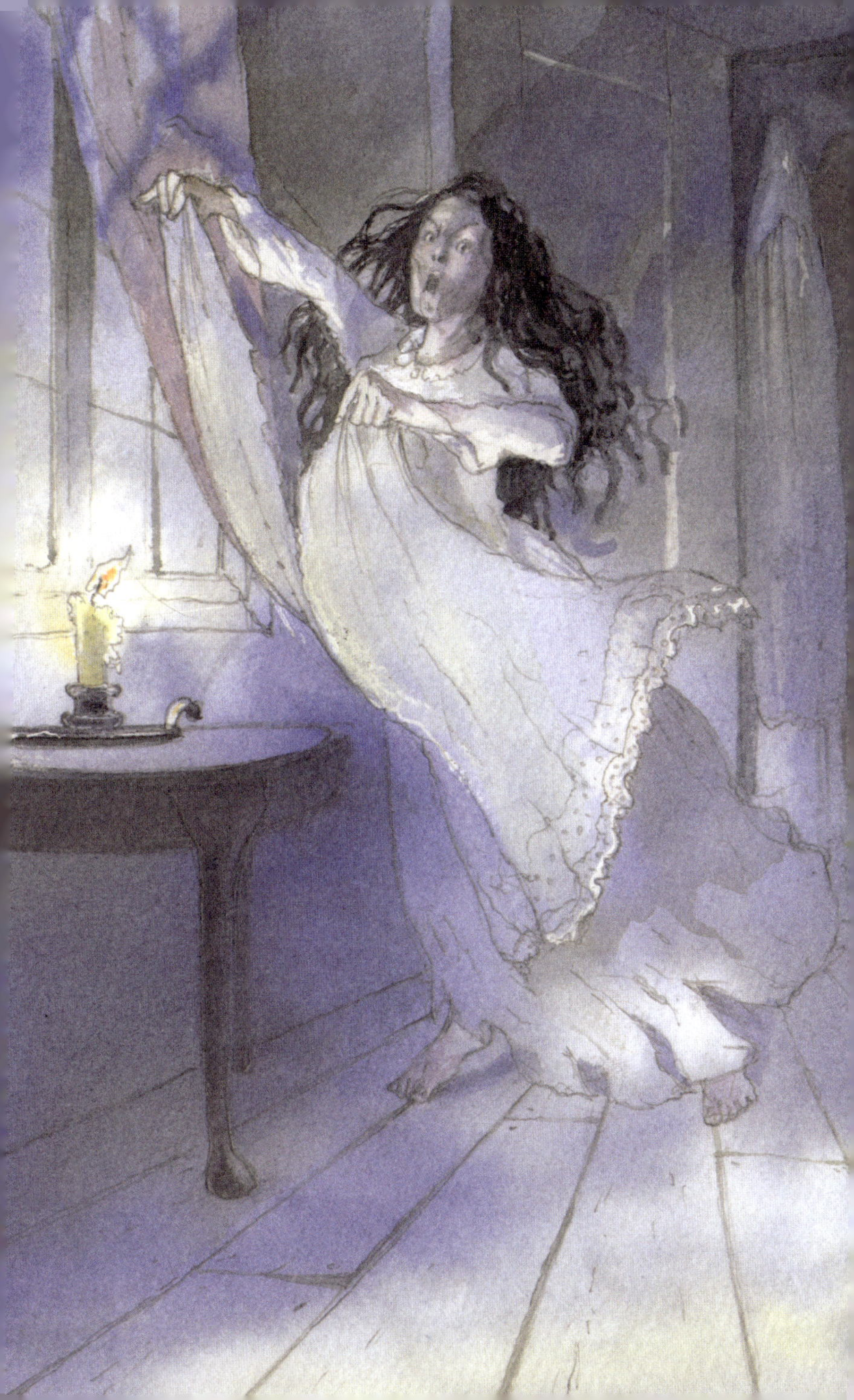

Ours was a simple wedding. At the church, the priest asked Mr. Rochester the age-old question, "Wilt thou have this woman to be thy wedded wife?"

From the back, a voice exclaimed: "The marriage cannot go on. Mr. Rochester has a wife already."

"What business is it of yours?" shouted Mr. Rochester, swinging around. "Go away!"

"I am a lawyer, sir, and I have a witness to your first marriage – a Mr. Mason, Mrs. Rochester's brother."

The visitor of a few weeks ago stepped forward. "I can prove that Mrs. Rochester is alive and living at Thornfield Hall."

"I never heard of her," stammered the clergyman.

"No, by heaven, I took care that none knew," raged Mr. Rochester. "It's true. I married Bertha Mason, fifteen years ago. She is crazy, she was always crazy, the daughter of three generations of maniacs. I was tricked into marrying her. Leave the church, everyone. There'll be no wedding today. Let us visit my charming wife, in the care of her keeper, Grace Poole."

In stunned silence, we returned to Thornfield, passed along the gallery, and climbed the stairs to the third floor. Mr. Rochester unlocked a door to reveal, in a windowless room, a growling figure on all fours, like a thick-maned animal. Startled, I recognized the purple, bloated face of the midnight visitor in my dream.

"Be careful, sir," warned Grace Poole. The creature sprang at Mr. Rochester's throat. He, wrestling, held her off.

"This is my wife. And this..." laying his hand on my shoulder, "...this quiet girl is what I wished to have. Judge me not, priest and lawyer. Leave me. I'll shut up my prize."

I slipped into my room, Jane Eyre, almost a bride, now a solitary girl again. Where was the girl of yesterday?

My hopes were gone, my love lost, my future void. I spent a miserable hour with bitter resolution. I had to leave.

I came out to find Mr. Rochester waiting. He seized me.

"Jane. Can you forgive me?"

Dear reader, I had already.

But when he tried to kiss me, I jerked away from him.

"What's this?" he demanded. "You won't kiss the husband of Bertha Mason?"

"I can't kiss anyone's husband," I said. "Let me go. Please don't be angry."

"I love you too much for anger," he said. "Don't you love me?"

"Of course I do."

"Then come away with me, abroad. We'll pretend you are my wife. No one will know."

"I can't live a lie," I insisted. "You have a wife."

"Jane," he begged. "I am not gentle-tempered. Don't try me like this. Don't fling me back to my old life, punished without end for the folly of my youth. Please come with me, my hope – my love – my life!"

He slumped against the wall in anguish, clenching his fists.

"God bless you. Farewell!" I said, stroking his arm... and left. In despair, I added to myself, "Farewell, forever." I had to go, before temptation overwhelmed me.

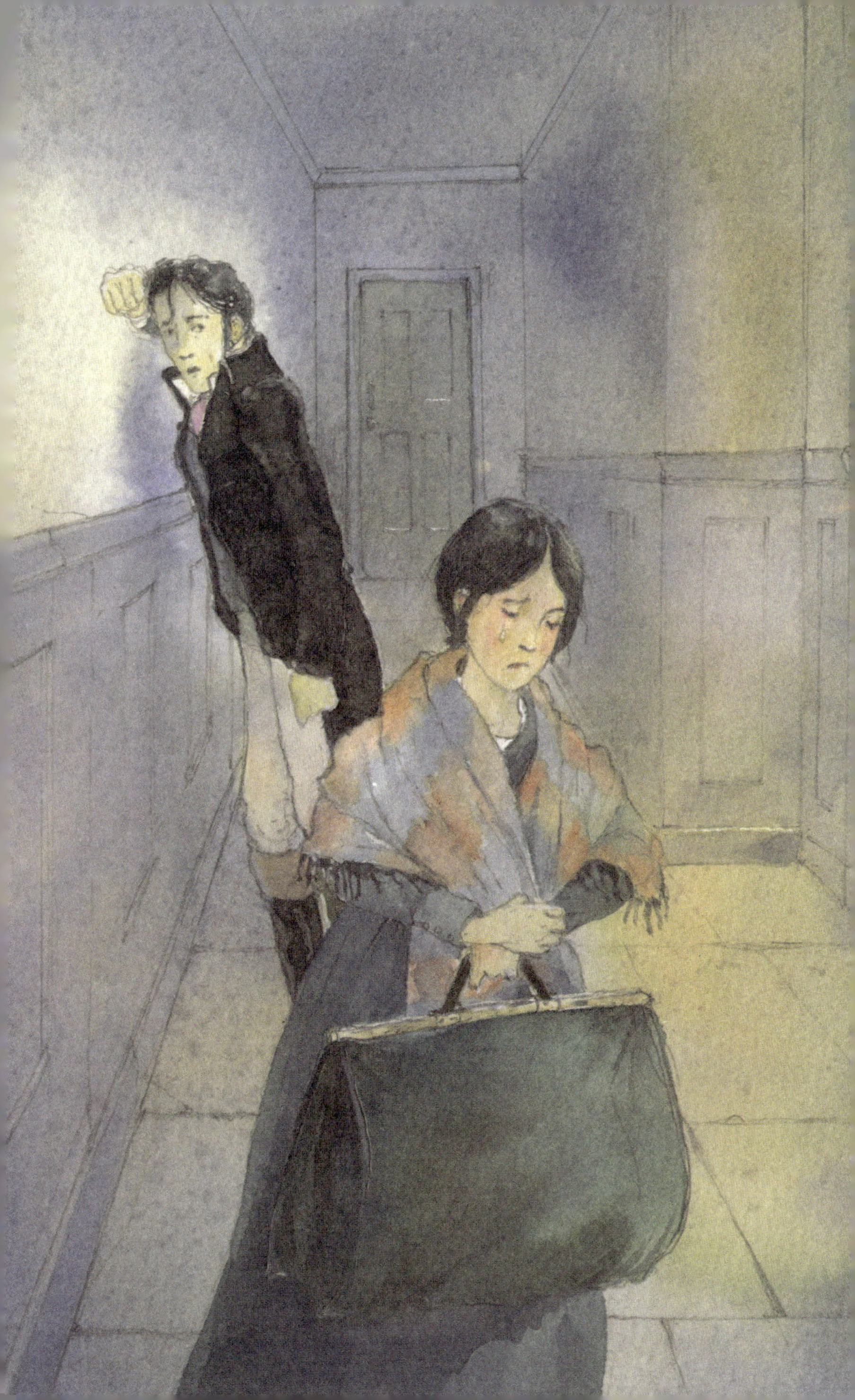

Oh, how I longed to be his comforter still. The thought of his unhappiness sickened me. Reader, may you never feel as I felt then.

I walked for hours. Finally, I saw a coach and jumped aboard, giving the driver all my money, in return for his promise to take me far away from Thornfield Hall.

Chapter 6

The voice from nowhere

Two days later I was in an unknown village. In my misery, I'd left my bag on the coach. I was truly destitute.

I walked on until nightfall. Drawing my shawl around me, I slept restlessly beneath a crag, shattered with longing for Mr. Rochester.

In the morning, weak with hunger, I found a village shop. "Does anyone here want a servant?" I asked.

"No."

"Is there any work hereabouts?"

"No."

Onwards again... I saw a child about to throw a mess of cold porridge into a pig trough.

"Please... give that to me," I pleaded and devoured it ravenously.

Exhausted, I stumbled on until I reached a cottage and knocked on the door. A young clergyman and two girls my own age opened it.

"Shelter," I gasped. "I beg you."

Reader, these kind strangers took me in, restored me to health, and found work for me as a teacher in the village school. They found it hard to understand my friendless state, without family, but they were sensitive, not inquisitive.

There I stayed. If I thought of the life I might have led, delirious with Mr. Rochester's love under foreign sunshine, pretending to be his wife, I knew at least that here I could be honest. I was grateful. I found my village pupils likeable, clever and anxious to learn.

And so my life passed, until one day...

That day I had the strangest feeling in my heart, sharp as an electric shock. Breathless, I waited and heard a voice cry:

"Jane! Jane! Jane!"

It came from nowhere, but I knew it at once – Edward Rochester's voice, in pain, desperate, eerie.

"I will come," I cried to the air. I gave in my notice at the school, bid my kind rescuers goodbye and caught a coach back to Thornfield.

How familiar and beloved it was! Past the lanes, through the fields, the house would come into view any moment now…

I saw a blackened, empty ruin.

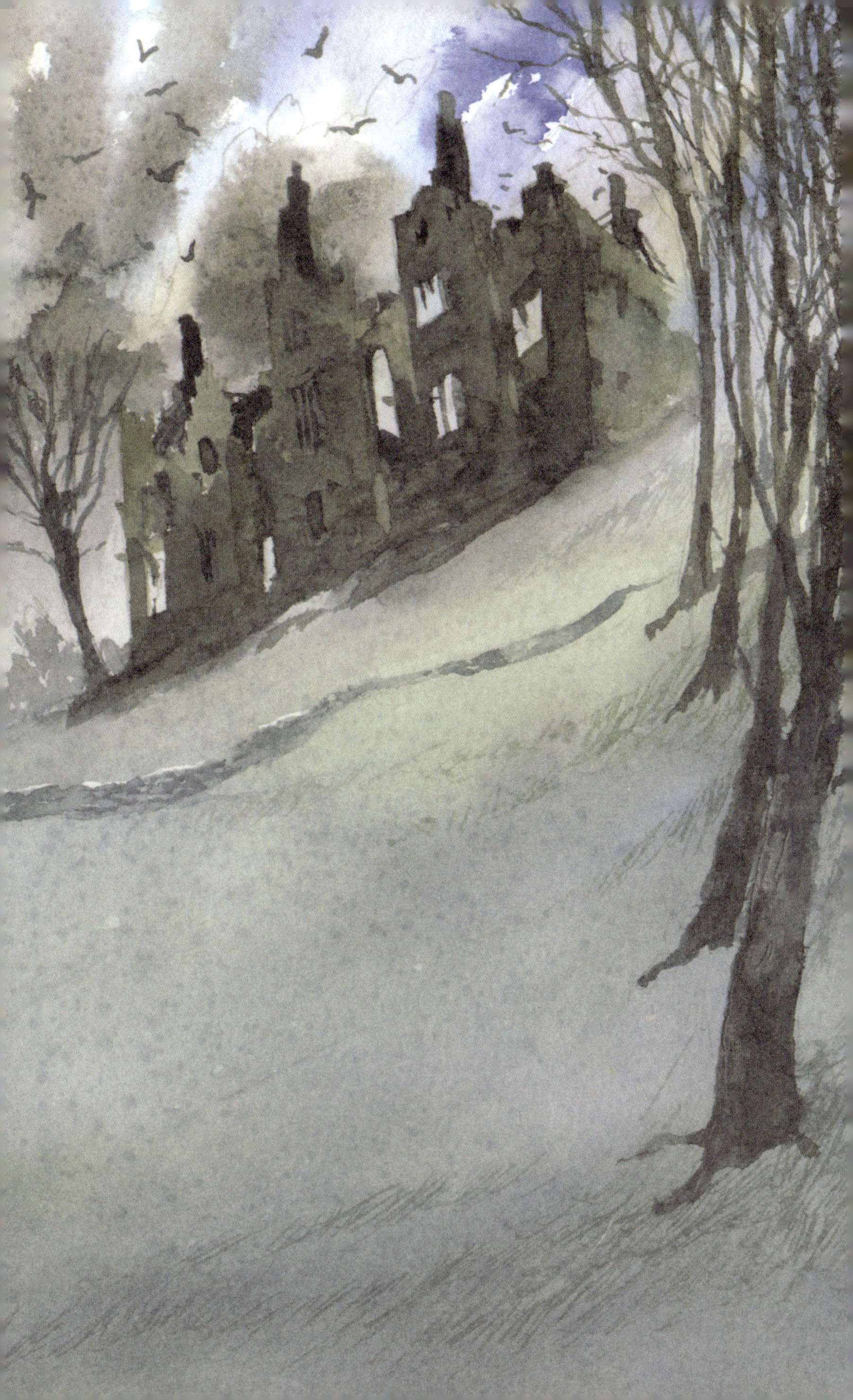

Distraught, I rushed to the nearest house. An old man answered my urgent questions.

"It was a fire in the dead of night," he said. "The lunatic started it, Mr. Rochester's secret wife. I saw her on the roof, waving her arms, a big woman with long black hair streaming against the flames. Mr. Rochester went to rescue her, but she yelled and jumped to her death on the ground."

"And HE?" I could hardly bear it. "Is he dead or alive?"

"Oh he's alive, but he's blind."

"Where is he?"

"At a farmhouse he owns, thirty miles away. They say he's a broken man."

I went to the farmhouse that very day. The place felt deserted, as though no one lived there. Inside, I found Mr. Rochester, utterly changed, not in his looks which were as strong as ever, but his countenance which was desolate, brooding, like a caged eagle.

"Who is it?" he asked, hearing footsteps.

Gently I asked, "Would you like some water?"

"What sweet madness is this?" He groped at the air, catching and seizing my hands. "Here are her fingers, small and slight... Is it you, Jane?"

"It is," I said. "I've come back to you. All my heart is yours, forever."

A tear trickled down his cheek. "No. You must not tie yourself to a scarred, blinded ruin."

"You're no ruin, you're strong," I comforted him.

"Oh Jane, if you knew how I've longed for you. One day, sick with misery, I called aloud, 'Jane! Jane! Jane!' 'I will come!' I seemed to hear you say. Thank God you are here."

Reader, I married him.

Adèle, I found, had been sent to school. Her joy at seeing me again moved me so much, I took her home with me.

Mr. Rochester continued blind for two years, until one day he said, "Jane, are you wearing a glittering necklace?"

"I am."

"And a blue dress?"

"Yes!"

His sight was returning, and when he held his first-born in his arms, he saw the boy had inherited his own eyes as they once were, large, brilliant and black.

Charlotte Brontë
1816-1855

Charlotte Brontë was one of six children. She and her brother and sisters loved writing, making up imaginary worlds for their stories.

When she was eight, Charlotte was sent away to school. She hated it and the school later appeared as Mr. Brocklehurst's school in *Jane Eyre*. Like Jane, Charlotte was a teacher and then a governess, but she dreamed of being a writer and, in 1847, *Jane Eyre* was published.

Charlotte's sisters, Emily and Anne, also became famous writers, and the Brontës' home at Haworth Parsonage is now a museum.

Haworth Parsonage, Yorkshire, England